This
book
belongs to:

Zachariah W.

Great Tales from Long Ago
KING MIDAS AND HIS GOLD

Retold by Catherine Storr
Illustrated by Mike Codd

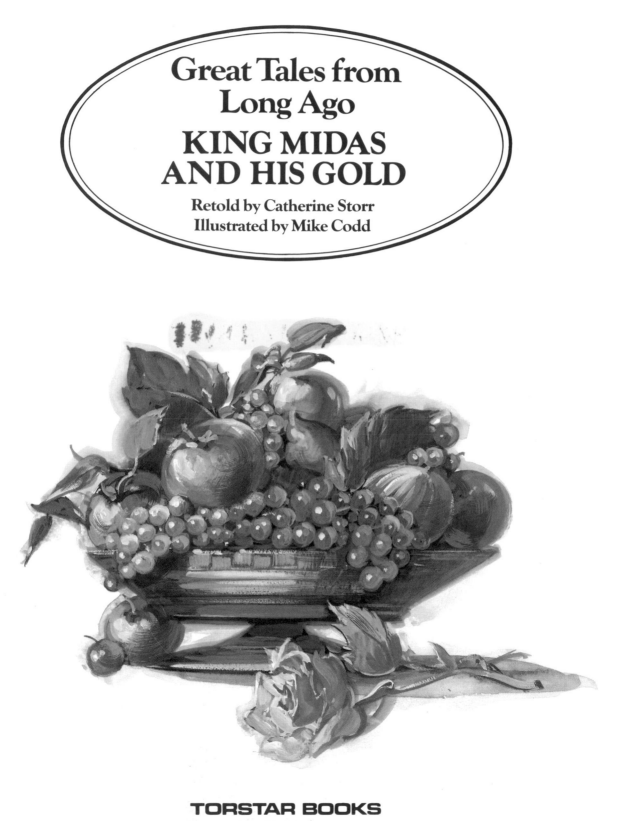

TORSTAR BOOKS

NEW YORK · TORONTO

GREAT TALES FROM LONG AGO
KING MIDAS AND HIS GOLD

Torstar Books Inc, 41 Madison Avenue, Suite 2900,
New York, NY 10010 by arrangement with Belitha Press Ltd.
Copyright © in this format Belitha Press Ltd, 1986
Text copyright © Catherine Storr, 1985
Illustrations copyright © Mike Codd, 1985
 Conceived and designed by Belitha Press Ltd,
2 Beresford Terrace, London N5 2DH.

Library of Congress Cataloging in Publication Data
Storr, Catherine.
King Midas and his gold.

(Great tales from long ago)
Originally published under title: King Midas.
Milwaukee: Raintree Children's Books, 1985.
Summary: A king who wishes for the golden touch
is faced with its unfortunate consequences.
1. Midas – Juvenile literature. [1. Midas.
2. Mythology, Greek] I. Codd, Michael, ill.
II. Title. III. Series.
BL820.M55S76   1986   398.2′2   85-28900

ISBN 1-55001-036-0 (Great Tales from Long Ago Series)
ISBN 1-55001-022-0 (King Midas and his Gold)
10 9 8 7 6 5 4 3 2
Printed in Belgium

Note: The source for the story is *The Greek
Myths* by Robert Graves.

CS

ONCE UPON A TIME THERE WAS A KING CALLED MIDAS.
He was very rich.
He lived in a marble palace decorated with gold.
He had a golden throne to sit on
and a golden crown to wear on his head.

HE HAD CHESTS FULL OF TREASURES,
golden necklaces, golden bracelets, and golden rings.
In side his palace he had trees made by clever craftsmen,
with gold and silver leaves.
The fruit that hung from the branches
was made of precious jewels.
Emerald and ruby, amethyst and topaz and lapis lazuli.

ONE DAY, THE MEN WHO WORKED IN MIDAS' GARDEN
found an old, shabby man asleep among the rose bushes.
They tied his hands and feet with garlands of roses,
and carried him as their prisoner to King Midas.

"Who are you? And what are you doing in my garden?"
Midas asked the man.
"Great King, the god of wine, Dionysus
has many followers.
I am one of them.
I am old Silenus.
If you will set me free
so that I can join him again,
I will tell you the most wonderful stories you have ever heard."

MIDAS KEPT SILENUS IN HIS PALACE FOR FIVE DAYS AND NIGHTS,
and he listened to his stories.
"I will tell you," said Silenus,
"how there is a great land, far away beyond the sea.
It is full of splendid cities,
and the people who live there are happy and tall
and they live nearly forever.
Or shall I tell you about the terrible whirlpool
which no human has ever been able to cross?

Nearby are two streams,
and on the banks of the streams
grow two different kinds of tree.
The man who eats the fruit of the first kind
becomes miserable and he cries and groans
until he dies. The man who eats the fruit
of the second kind of tree grows younger every day.
Even old men can become babies again.''

AFTER HEARING THESE STORIES, MIDAS LET SILENUS GO.
The god Dionysus sent a message to Midas.
"I will reward you for looking after my old friend.
Tell me what your dearest wish is and I will grant it."
Midas said at once, "I should like best
that everything I touch should turn into gold."

"Think carefully what you are asking for," Dionysus said.
But Midas would not stop to think.
He wanted to be the richest man in the world.
Dionysus said, "Then I will grant your wish.
From now on, you have the Golden Touch."

MIDAS WAS DELIGHTED
He touched the stone bench in the garden.
It immediately turned into gold.
He picked up a pebble from the ground,
and found that he held a nugget of gold.

"Wonderful! I shall have a golden palace!
I will have a forest of golden trees!
Everything around me will be made of gold!" Midas said.
He went around his palace and his garden,
turning stone and wood and marble into gold.
The roses now had heavy golden blossoms and leaves,
on golden stems stiff with golden thorns.

PRESENTLY MIDAS WAS HUNGRY AND THIRSTY.
He went into his palace and sat at his table.
He called to his servants to bring him a cup of wine.
He was delighted when he saw
that as his fingers touched the cup,
it turned into a golden goblet.

But as his tongue tasted the wine,
that, too, turned into solid gold.

"Bring me food!" he commanded.
His cooks brought their choicest dishes
and set them before him.
·But when the meat and the bread reached his mouth,
they became gold, as hard as stone.
He took a peach from the golden tray,
and it lay heavy and cold in his hand.

"Alas! I have been a fool!
I have asked for the Golden Touch,
and now, even though I am the richest man in the world,
I must die of hunger and thirst!" said Midas.
He called out to the god, Dionysus. He said,
"Great god! You were right and I was wrong.
Forgive me! Take back your gift!"

Dionysus laughed. But he was sorry for King Midas.
He told him, "Go and wash in the river
and you will be free from the Golden Touch.
Then everything that has changed will become
itself again."

THE TREES SWAYED IN THE WIND.
The flowers smelled sweet. Midas ate a huge meal.
He enjoyed the red wine and the good bread.

He was very happy now,
even though he was no longer
the richest man in the world.